dreamers

THE GIRL WHO LOVED TO SING

This book belongs to

Read more in the Dreamers series by
Lavanya Karthik

The Boy Who Played with Light: Satyajit Ray

dreamers

THE GIRL WHO LOVED TO SING

TEEJAN BAI

LAVANYA KARTHIK

duckbill

An imprint of Penguin Random House

For you, with a song in your heart

PENGUIN BOOKS

USA | Canada | UK | Ireland | Australia
New Zealand | India | South Africa | China | Singapore

Duckbill Books is part of the Penguin Random House group of companies
whose addresses can be found at global.penguinrandomhouse.com

Published by Penguin Random House India Pvt. Ltd
4th Floor, Capital Tower 1, MG Road,
Gurugram 122 002, Haryana, India

Penguin
Random House
India

First published in Duckbill Books by
Penguin Random House India 2021

Text and illustrations copyright © Lavanya Karthik 2021

All rights reserved

10 9 8 7 6 5 4

This book is, as the author claims, a work of 'faction' and, while fixed both historically
and chronologically, remains fiction, based on fact, embroidered and distorted in order
to project the character herein. All names, save where obviously genuine, are fictitious
and any resemblance to persons living or dead is wholly coincidental.

ISBN 9780143451518

Typeset in Georgia by DiTech Publishing Services Pvt. Ltd
Printed at Aarvee Promotions, India

www.penguin.co.in

A vast auditorium, filled with people, waits.

A woman steps out on to the stage.

The audience murmurs.

The harmonium starts up a tune. The dholak adds a beat, the tabla keeps pace, the khartal follows.

Sa na na na na na na moha!

It is a song of sadness and struggle, of hardship and pain.

It is a story from the Mahabharata.

But it could just as well be her own.

In the village of Ganiyari, a baby girl is born.

No smiles greet her, no songs ring out to celebrate her arrival.

'We can barely feed ourselves,' Ma grumbles. 'What will we feed her?'

'Her body is weak,' say the village elders. 'Her heart barely beats; her voice is a mere whisper. You will soon be rid of her.'

The elders are wrong.

Teejan lives. She grows. She thrives!

Her heart beats strong and steady. Her body grows straight and tall.

And her voice? Her voice is the strongest of all.

Teejan sings!

She sings as she cooks and cleans.

She sings as she tends to her little brothers and sisters, sending them off to school while she stays home.

She sings as she weaves mats and brooms to sell in the market.

'Girls do not sing in our family!' Ma scolds.

Teejan sings!

When she is up in the trees, which she climbs faster and higher than anyone else in the village.

When she is out in the field, playing kabaddi with the village boys.

When Ma locks her away without food and water, to teach her to stay quiet.

Teejan sings!

Jhunjhuni!

The first time Teejan hears her grandfather Brijlal recite Pandvani, she feels a thrill like an electric current. He tells stories of the lives of the Pandava princes from the Mahabharata.

Pagalpana!

A madness takes hold of her, as she sneaks away each night to listen to Brijlal,

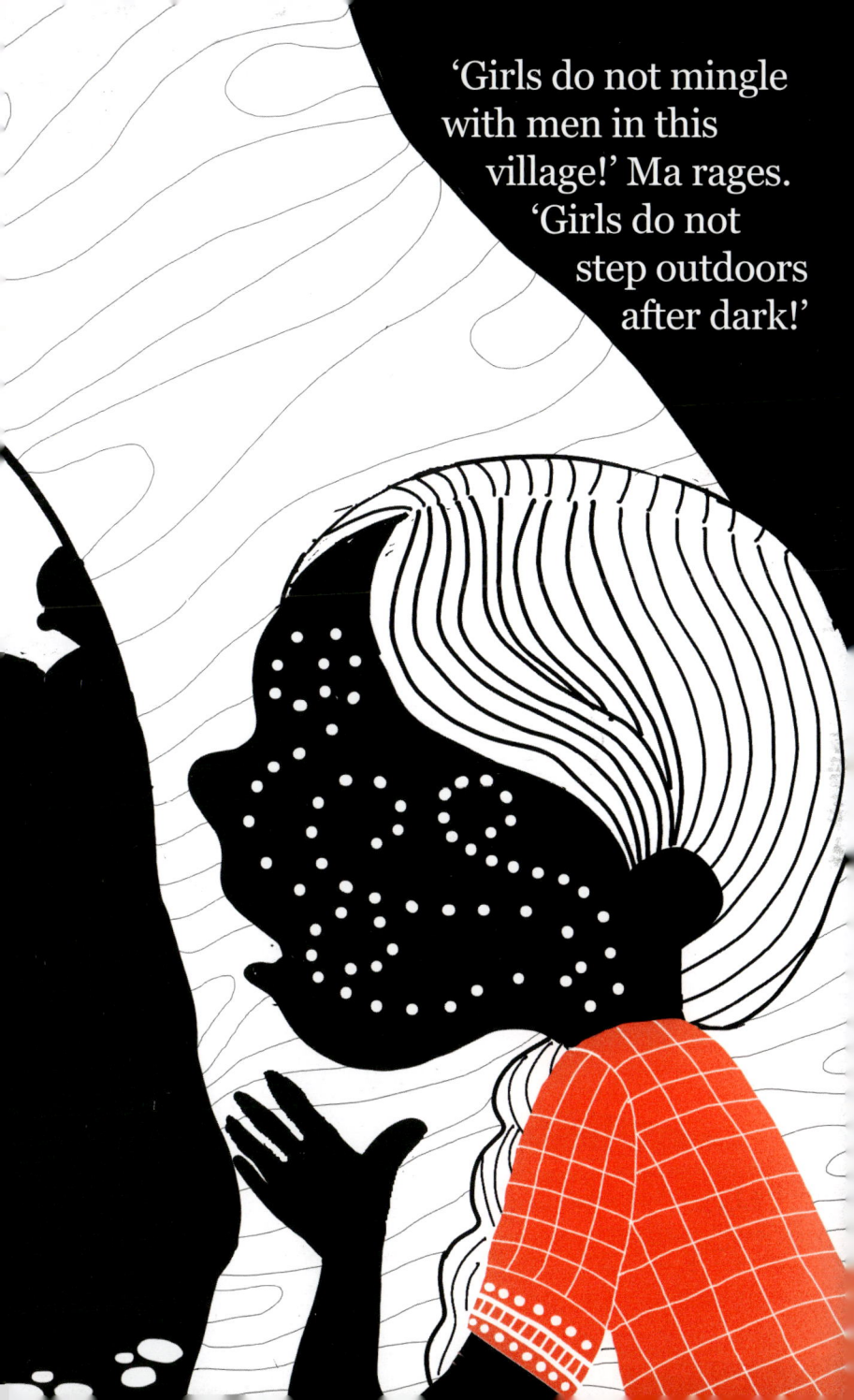

'Girls do not mingle with men in this village!' Ma rages. 'Girls do not step outdoors after dark!'

Teejan is married off at twelve, and sent away.

'This will teach her to be silent,' Ma says.

'This should take the pagalpana out of her,' the village elders smile.

The elders are wrong.

Pagalpana!

Teejan comes back home,
determined to sing.

Jhunjhuni!

It keeps her strong when the village
shuns and taunts her.

Brijlal is touched by her spirit.
'Would you like me to teach you?'
he asks.

Once again, Teejan sneaks out after her chores for lessons with her grandfather.

Brijlal gives her her first tanpura. 'Become your characters! Become your story!'

'Feel the music!

'Feel the story!

'Feel it come alive!'

Teejan sings!

'Don't just sing—become the song!

'Become the characters in it!'

Teejan sings!

Teejan cannot eat, she cannot sleep! All she can think of is song.

She forgets her chores; she ignores her siblings, until one day, Ma catches her singing . . .

Teejan runs away.

In the neighbouring village of Chandkhuri, she builds herself a hut and makes a living by weaving mats.

And as she weaves, she sings.

It is not long before her voice is heard.

That evening, a crowd gathers
before a makeshift stage. Teejan steps
on to the stage.

'A mere girl singing Pandvani!'
the crowd murmurs.

Teejan stands tall.

Become your characters.

Feel the story, she tells herself.

Jhunjhuni!

Pagalpana!

Sa na na na na na moha!

Teejan sings!
One by one, the murmurs die out.

Every evening for fifteen days, Teejan sings before the people of Chandkhuri.

By the last day, her fame spreads well beyond the village.

Teejan had left home, penniless and unwanted.

She returned home, a singer and a legend.

The song ends. The audience roars with applause.

Teejan's song may have begun with sadness and struggle, but it ends with happiness and victory, with prosperity and plentifulness. It is a tale of hope, of endurance, of courage against all odds.

It is a story from the Mahabharata.

But it could just as well be her own.

Teejan Bai was born on 8 August 1956 in the village of Ganiyari, near Bhilai, present-day Chhattisgarh. Her parents, who were Pardhi Bhil tribals, wove reed mats and collected honey for a living.

Teejan went on to become the world's foremost Pandvani performer, travelling across the globe to sing before prime ministers and queens, film stars and schoolchildren. She was also the first woman to sing Pandvani in the dramatic 'kapalik' style, rather than the more sedate 'vedamati' style expected of women.

She was showered with honours and awards, including the Padma Shri, Padma Vibhushan, Sangeet Natak Akademi Award and the Fukuoka Prize.

To this day, she lives in Ganiyari. And each time she sings for an audience, she still feels . . . Jhunjhuni! Pagalpana!

The illustrations in this book are inspired by the rich and vibrant art of the Bhils.

Lavanya Karthik is an author by day, a cookie monster by teatime and fast asleep by nine every night. She lives in Mumbai, where she writes, draws, eats a lot of chocolate and takes a lot of naps.